BRIDGING THE GAP

Nicholas Duncan-Williams

BRIDGING
THE
GAP

ISBN: 978-9988-8646-9-9

Printed and in Ghana by
Type Company Limited
P.O. Box 854, Kaneshie
Accra, Ghana
Tel. +233 30.223.2252
Email: type@africaonline.com.gh

Table of Contents

INTRODUCTION

Imagine spending all your resources and energy in a life time climbing a mountain only to reach the top and realize you have climbed the wrong mountain?

How catastrophic and regretful can that be? These are the hard and harsh realities that constantly must inform and guide our journeys through life.

There are clearly defined ways by the master navigator and foundation laid in place by the master builder upon which we must all build in order to ensure a lasting and a guaranteed future

The scriptures declare that wisdom and knowledge shall be the stability of our time.

The older generation has wisdom, the younger generation has knowledge. When the two find commonality and are fused together, that is when stability, which is non negotiable, comes.

The recognition by the church of the role the young generation must play is critical for the future survival of God's agenda on earth.

just as it is done in the family setting. Mothers must at a point begin to teach their daughters basic survival life principles instead of they sitting all the time for things to be done for them. Fathers at a certain point must train their sons to play some of their roles so there will be continuity in the communities.

Observing the current trend of mutual suspicions of mistrust between the old and the young generation, across a broad spectrum of our societies, create a dangerous disconnect that endangers the future.

A careful look from the perspective of scripture about those who took advantage of the good counsel of the elderly and the good it led to vis a vis those who neglected the wise counsel of his father's Counsellors, Jeroboam in this case, led to the loss of ten out of the twelve tribes of Israel.

These sorts of happenings if left unchecked can lead to disastrous consequences

This book seeks to address the gap and put forward suggestions that will call upon the old and young generation to bridge the gap to ensure continuity, progress, development and longevity.

This will prevent a shipwreck and collapse of what has been built and we are building upon.

At all cost, avoid the curse, which is basically the destruction of all that we have labored to build.

DEDICATION

From the very depth of my heart I dedicate this book to the old and current generation who are working tirelessly with the young and emerging generation in mind.

May your legacies not perish but be established in the name of Jesus Christ.

CHAPTER 1

Mind the Gap

Each generation will reap what the former generation has sown. – An Ancient Proverb.

In order to bridge the gap between young and old, parents and children, and one generation to the next, we must understand what a gap entails, and mind the gap.

The British people frequently use the expression "mind the gap," when someone is exiting the subway or train door. The phrase serves as a warning to prevent passengers from missing the platform and stepping into the "gap" or space between the train and the platform. In this instance, a gap is defined as a break or opening, an empty space or interval, interruption in continuity, or wide divergence or difference. However, a gap can also be a disparity in attitudes, perceptions, character, or development, or a lack of confidence or understanding, perceived as creating a problem.

Today there are disparities in attitudes, values, ethics, character, and perceptions between the established generation of leaders, mothers, and fathers, and the emerging generation. Many in the emerging or younger generation view those who are older as archaic, out-of-touch, intolerant, and unbothered. Despite being right or wrong, the younger generation's perception of the established generation's approach is often dictatorial. This approach and communication style turns off the younger generation and prevents them from legitimately sharing their point of view.

As a result, the older generation is preparing a future for their children instead of preparing their children for the future. Much energy is spent on labor and prosperity, but fewer opportunities to impart the wisdom necessary for its maintenance and longevity. It is said that "hard times create strong men, strong men create easy times, easy times create weak men, and weak men create hard times." If we fail to bridge the gap to receive and impart wisdom, weak men and hard times will become the norm.

The other side of the gap is that many in the older generation view the youth as disloyal and entitled. They are irritated when they see those in the emerging generation who believe they can have what the fathers have received over the years easily, by osmosis, or through the laying on of hands, without years of character development. Youth and inexperience cause the younger generation to proverbially cry out, "I want your anointing man (or woman) of God! Lay hands on me!" In fact, some care nothing about impartation, but think their accumulation of material possessions is enough to qualify them to "rub shoulders" with mothers and fathers, when they have not yet been tested and tried. Gold is not gold until it is tested by fire. There is a lack of honor and appreciation for the pain, trials, and perseverance of the older generation which furthers the gap.

Yet, if each generation stands resolute on their respective sides, unwilling to reach out to the other to address the disparities, everyone loses. The polarities that exist today... extremism and the unwillingness to bridge the gap is one of the most dangerous mindsets plaguing our societies. The difference is reflected in the widening gap between rich and poor, religious organizations and political parties as well as the gap between both generations.

This is not a recent phenomenon. It is something that has fought many generations since biblical times and throughout history. Each generation must desire a win-win outcome. To bridge the gap, each generation must have a change of heart. Malachi 4:6 tells us that God wants us to reconcile, restore, build a bridge, or bridge the gap between generations.

> *And he shall turn the heart of the fathers to the children, and the heart of the children to their fathers, lest I come and smite the earth with a curse.*
>
> *(Malachi 4:6 KJV)*

\Several generations, including baby boomers, live on the earth today. And each generation represents a different era, way of thinking, and set of values.

Year Born/Generation:	Age in 2022:
Gen Zers: 1999 and after	18 to 21
Younger Gen Y/Millennials: 1990-1998	22 to 30
Older Gen Y/Millennials: 1980-1989	31 to 40
Gen Xers: 1965-1979	41 to 55
Younger Boomers: 1955-1964	56 to 65
Older Boomers: 1946-1954	66 to 74
Silent Generation: 1925-1945	75 to 95

Source: Census.gov

We must understand that both generations have something to learn from each other. If they fail to connect and relate to each other in the proper manner, something will be lost. What we call a generational gap is usually a result of an interaction gap.

By grace of God, I maintained connection with the fathers like Morris Cerullo, T.L. Osborne, Archbishop Benson Idahosa, Dr. Oral Roberts, and Dr. Lester Sumrall to name a few. We were from different generations and different cultures. Yet I have reaped more than I sowed from these strategic relationships. Through their wisdom, correction, and impartation, I have become a better father because I stood on their shoulders. Sir Isaac Newton, the famous English scientist, once said, "If I have seen further, it is by standing on the shoulders of giants." They didn't always say things in a nice way or even say what I wanted to hear but I remained teachable. I honored the generation that went before me, and it continues to make a difference in my life, relationships, and ministry today.

> *Hearken to me, ye that follow after righteousness, ye that seek the Lord: look unto the rock whence ye are hewn, and to the hole of the pit whence ye are digged.*
>
> *(Isaiah 51:1 KJV)*

I want the same for the next generation. I am very concerned that if we don't bridge the gap for families, nations, businesses, and ministries, the next generation will be ill-prepared for what's in front of them, whether in business, ministry, or education, we need to bridge the gap to ensure the strength of the next generation of leaders, educators, fathers, and mothers. The gaps begin in our mindsets. To bridge the gap, we must deal with mindsets.

Mindset Gaps: Parallel Worldviews

There are indeed marked differences in generational mindsets because mindsets are, at least in part, shaped by the times. Each generation has its own way of looking at things that can easily cause conflict or mistrust if not considered in the light of wisdom and proper perspective. For example, in the past it was common to work for one company for thirty or forty years. Today, Millennials and Gen Zers view working for one company for that long as a limitation. It is not even an expectation nor desire, because the world is significantly more mobile now.

There has been a huge cultural shift in the context of a global village and information age of rapid technological innovation.

Technology is closing the gap between what one can imagine and what one can do. As a result, the equality of opportunity is unmatched in human history. – Matt Mullenweg

People relocate more frequently and therefore change jobs more frequently. The younger generation doesn't view this as an issue of loyalty, disloyalty, or entitlement but rather survival. However, someone from an older generation may see a millennial's frequent movement as a lack of loyalty without first considering or trying to educate them about what loyalty should look like in the present generation.

Technology is not a barrier for them but a necessity. They have grown up on social media, the Internet, and mobile devices. When it comes to technology, we can never go back to the way things used to be, and many fathers and mothers have not come to grips with that, and if they do not have relationships with younger people, they may not come to the necessary understanding. For example, the COVID pandemic impacted the way work gets done. Working from home is no longer an exception. It's a norm. Streaming online services is no longer something that is nice to do, but a necessity. It provides opportunities to touch many lives all over the world. The e emerging generation will see this as something normal, whereas the older generation may need significant effort to adjust.

Using technology is second nature to them. They can use their phones to create their own platforms. They are no longer compelled to wait around serving for years and years for the opportunity to stand in the older generation's pulpit. They can go on their phones and create their own pulpit, many times reaching more people through their phone and social media app than they would standing in our pulpits. So, we must have more to offer the emerging generation than the threat of not being able to preach. What wisdom are we imparting? How are we demonstrating the true mentoring hand of a father or mother?

Will the older generation crucify them for using technology or see it as disloyalty? Will we still expect them to do things the way we did it?

How will the established generation deal with this? Will we be apt to mentor and teach so they understand the blessings in serving another's vision before launching their own? We cannot just assume they understand these things.

How we communicate these issues to the younger generation is also important. There must be mutual understanding—understanding from both sides of the gap. The emerging generation is confronted with issues the older generation was not confronted with. When it comes to race, gender, family, work, and ethics, they are not being taught to do things the way the older generation did it. They have attended and will attend school with members of different religious beliefs or orientation, the LGBTQ community, teenage mothers and fathers, and the mentally ill, and are taught that topics the older generation shunned and saw as taboo must now be addressed.

So we must understand that bridging the gap between generations means bridging mindsets. The fathering and mothering generation must understand this to adopt a "trans-generational" mindset, communicate truth effectively, and not become angry when they see certain things in young(er) people.

Alone, we can do so little; together, we can do so much. – Helen Keller

There are older generations who have wisdom, experience, and lessons about the ancient landmarks of honor, sacrifice, loyalty, and more to teach the younger generations. Likewise, the younger generation have contributions to make. The Scripture says the glory of the young man is his strength, and the older generation sometimes criticizes the younger for their strength and zeal displayed without knowledge and wisdom. The older generation held Moses' hands up on the mountain while Joshua the younger generation fights in the valley. It takes both generations to win together.

The older generation must also remember that they will not lead forever, and without the younger generation, Moses would have had no successor. Leadership is a relay race not a marathon. At some point, every leader will need to pass the baton. If we fail to bridge the gap, we will lose potential successors and negatively affect the future of our churches, businesses, and nations. Together, we can do much for the kingdom and our nations if we bridge the gap and hold onto the ancient landmarks.

Love is what enables us to bridge the gap of disappointment when others don't live up to the expectations we have of them. - Abigail Van Buren

CHAPTER 2

Foundations: The God of Generations

True Leadership is having multiple generations working together successfully and passionately to create significance. *Farshad Asl*

The name Benny Hinn has become synonymous with the phrase "healing ministry." He runs an international non-profit ministry, has authored several books, has an international television broadcast, is one of the foremost pastors in the body of Christ, and his anointing and ministry has transcended decades. But what many do not realize is that his persistence and longevity in ministry has much to do with him having walked with those whose ministries existed before him.

God is a generational God: when he thinks, plans; and acts, it's never for the benefit of a sole individual. Some people think Benny Hinn just appeared out of nowhere one day, but he was shaped, formed, and impacted by many more-experienced men and women of God, fathers and mothers in the faith who belonged to the generations that preceded him.

This principle and character of God is one of his unique attributes which he wants his children and his people to adopt. For example, the Jewish culture is one of the most progressive in the world. In that culture, when making large purchases, the patriarchs of that culture usually think about how to pass it on to their children and grandchildren. A Jewish patriarch usually thinks about leaving an inheritance for his children's children. He is thinking about his child's future, from choosing their name to life insurances, homes, businesses, properties, and college tuition. They are all secured for when the child graduates from college along with a car or first house for when they get married.

The Jewish patriarch or matriarch lays a strong foundation for subsequent generations to do the same for those after them. Can you imagine your parents doing this for you, as opposed to having to struggle all through school with student loan debt after graduating—having to find a job, struggling for years to pay off a student loan, car note, and mortgage? Then, on top of all that, trying to save enough for retirement? How can anyone under such a load effectively think about the next generation? God never intended it to be this way. He wanted the blessings to continue from one generation to the next. He wanted it to be transgenerational.

God revealed Himself to Moses as the God of Abraham, Isaac, and Jacob. In the same way, when God makes Himself known to ministers today, there should be a point of reference.

Pastor Benny Hinn has a point of reference, he was not a "lone ranger" and did not disconnect from those who trained, mentored, and groomed him.

I had occasion to speak with Pastor Benny about his experiences and encounters with some of the patriarchs and matriarchs, choice servants, and generals that have gone ahead of us. I am going to share some of that dialog from our conversation later in this chapter.

He had the opportunity and privilege to serve, learn, walk with, and be mentored by great servants of God, to encounter their anointing and presence. He is an embodiment of so many men and women of God that have gone ahead of our generation. He touched them and they touched and impacted him.

There was transgenerational impartation, which would have never happened if there had been a gap between them.

Years ago, Pastor Benny Hinn came to Ghana for the first time to run a crusade. Around the same time, my son Joel and I were traveling with Dr. Lester Sumrall and arrived in Amsterdam at Schiphol Airport. Dr. Sumrall was leaving to board his next flight. Joel and I were going to London, and he was going to Chicago. The Lord said to me, "You will not see him again, so ask him to bless you." So I approached him and said, "Papa, Papa, you need to bless me." He turned back and laid his hands on my shoulders, and said, "Let the anointing and the power of God that rests upon me, rest upon this young man. And God, keep him, keep him, keep him from harm's way and let your mantle be strong upon him." He prayed such a powerful prayer that day. I felt God's anointing so strong that sometimes when I preach, I can still hear his voice coming through me.

Benny Hinn also walked with fathers like Archbishop Benson Idahosa who impacted both of our lives in diverse ways. Sometimes, I will be preaching, and I will sense the mantle of Archbishop Idahosa on me.

I remember the rock from whence I was hewn. I had the privilege to serve and I am standing on the shoulders of giants like T.L. Osborne, Oral Roberts, Morris Cerullo, Papa Hagin, Dr. Lester Sumrall, and Papa Benson Idahosa of blessed memory.

When we read through the Bible, there are numerous accounts that reveal God's system, principle, and wisdom as a transgenerational God. He revealed himself to Moses as the God of Abraham, Isaac, and Jacob. In his appearance to Abraham and his promises to him, he also made the promise to his seed after him.

> *And in thy seed shall all the nations of the earth be blessed; because thou hast obeyed my voice.*
>
> *(Genesis 22:18 KJV)*

Then, he spoke to Isaac and reiterated the blessing:

And there was a famine in the land, beside the first famine that was in the days of Abraham. And Isaac went unto Abimelech king of the Philistines unto Gerar. And the Lord appeared unto him, and said, Go not down into Egypt; dwell in the land which I shall tell thee of: 3 Sojourn in this land, and I will be with thee, and will bless thee; for unto thee, and unto thy seed, I will give all these countries, and I will perform the oath which I sware unto Abraham thy father; 4 And I will make thy seed to multiply as the stars of heaven, and will give unto thy seed all these countries; and in thy seed shall all the nations of the earth be blessed; 5 Because that Abraham obeyed my voice, and kept my charge, my commandments, my statutes, and my laws. (Genesis 26:1-5 KJV)

Later, he spoke to Jacob, to again reiterate the blessing:

> *And God appeared unto Jacob again, when he came out of Padanaram, and blessed him. And God said unto him, Thy name is Jacob: thy name shall not be called any more Jacob, but Israel shall be thy name: and he called his name Israel. And God said unto him, I am God Almighty: be fruitful and multiply; a nation and a company of nations shall be of thee, and kings shall come out of thy loins; And the land which I gave Abraham and Isaac, to thee I will give it, and to thy seed after thee will I give the land. And God went up from him in the place where he talked with him.*
>
> *(Genesis 35:9-13 KJV)*

God's promise had been rehearsed in Isaac and Jacob's hearing for generations. They had seen their father sacrifice, heard God's voice, and obeyed Him. They had learned the ancient landmarks by observation and through relationship. That is one of the benefits of transgenerational connectedness and sonship. What they saw compelled them to work and set the stage for generations that would come after them. Likewise, there are so many things I observed in the life of Archbishop Benson Idahosa that affect the way I work and operate today. That is the way God designed it. That is why one of the biggest mistakes any generation can make is to ignore the generation that was before them.

> *One generation shall praise thy works to another, and shall declare thy mighty acts.*
>
> *(Psalm 145:4 KJV)*

Pastor Benny and I once had a conversation about the generation that came before us. It holds great insight for current and emerging generations. In it, the importance of strong foundations and wisdom for all generations are revealed. Here are a few highlights from that conversation.

Me: I sat and heard you. You were so real, practical, and vulnerable and brought us all back to the message of the Cross, which this generation knows nothing about. And we can't blame them. I think that we preachers must take responsibility for the fact that we've been so involved in trying to be big and not great, because everybody can be big but not everybody can be great. I mean I see you as great. Not big but great because longevity produces greatness and going through the process and being tested and tried like you have, those are the things that produce greatness, which this generation doesn't know. We have a generation that wants to make it overnight. Success and numbers are what drives this generation. But you are coming from a different generation, and I think that we need to hear from you about your experience of walking with some of the fathers. And people like the testimony you gave about Kathryn Kuhlman and Mr. Pentecost. I got to know about Mr. Pentecost and so many of the fathers and I believe that this generation needs to know about them and then we want to also, later, in this conversation, ask you about their children. What has become of their kids. Are they walking with God? What has become of their legacy? This will help this generation to learn. A great man of God, (I won't mention his name), came to me one time. He flew here in his jet and he drove straight to my office. He said, what's going on with our kids?" What's happening? And I said, it's a battle over the next generation - the legacy. The enemy so hates us that he doesn't want our seed after us to walk the face of the earth and we need to put up a fight to secure the next generation and our legacy, so that when we are gone, we will have another generation more anointed than we are, better than us, because we fought and we broke the ground and secured the next generation.

Pastor Benny: Well, I do want to talk about the Cross because that's something I think is so important today. The world has always been an evil place. Today the world has become intensely evil because of social media, because of the change and people's hunger. You know, when I got saved in the early seventies, it was a whole different world. And I worry about my children, I worry about my grandchildren especially. What kind of world would they have? But the message of Calvary is the only answer to the future. And when we talk about Calvary and the Cross most people probably do not realize what I mean. The Cross is a daily experience with us. Daily experience where our will must submit to the will of God.

What we want in life is not important. It's what the Lord wants in life. And often His will and our will cross each other. And what God is asking of us can be very difficult. But not if we love Him. Nothing then is difficult. What we have got to be so careful with, Archbishop, is we cannot allow the world to pollute our hearts at all. We have to detach ourselves....

Me: ... we can't conform. We have to transform.

Pastor Benny: ... we can never conform to the world. Yeah. So it's an ongoing daily battle. When I started as a Christian that was the message I heard from the greats - all the greats.

Please remember, Pastor Benny said, "The Cross is a daily experience with us—a daily experience where our will must submit to the will of God." If the foundation of our motives and ministries is not the Cross, we are in trouble. Our ultimate calling is to the fellowship of his sufferings; many young preachers and emerging leaders don't want to embrace that, but it's the only sure foundation—the Cross. Let's continue with more of the conversation.

Pastor Benny: Do you know the name Richard Wurmbrand who was a mighty saint of God? I will never forget looking at that man's face shining when he was ministering, talking about how he suffered in Siberia where the Soviet soldiers put him in a pit in winter naked for three weeks, wanting to kill them. And how they lowered the barriers into this pit in Siberia and put nails in the pit so if they would lean the nails would go into their [prisoners] body, and no food, no water, no warmth for three weeks. And the soldiers will come and mock them. They could not kill them. Finally, when they took them out, not one of them was hungry, not one of them was cold. They could not kill them. Oh yeah, this is an amazing thing. And imagine being exposed to that message.

Me: Pastor Benny, what has changed, looking at where you've come from in the early seventies to now, when it comes to the message and the fact that we don't hear about the message of the Cross and suffering - the baptism of suffering. We don't hear about suffering anymore.

Pastor Benny: Oh, my goodness, wow! Well, all who live godly will suffer persecution. That's in the Bible. Today nobody wants to talk about that. But that's all that we heard back then from people like Basilea Schlink. Basilea Schlink was one of the most amazing saints in Germany and had a great influence, still does through the Sisterhood of Mary they are called in Darmstadt. And the same thing we heard from so many in those days. I mean Kathryn Kuhlman, that's all she would talk about. But not just these women. A lot of men preached it. David du Plessis' message was forgiveness. He would cry and beg people to forgive. That's the Cross. Look at Billy Graham. What did he preach? The Cross. And he shook the world. So the message of the Cross simply is the message of surrender to the Lord - complete yieldedness to the Lord. You know, the Christian faith does not say try. Or try again. When it comes to our walk, God did not say to us, try to live it. He said, yield. The word in the Bible is not try or try again or struggle, it's yield.

Me: Surrender.

Pastor Benny: Surrender. That's the message of Calvary. That we surrender. It says yield your bodies. Surrender your life. Surrender to the Lord. Today we don't hear that. What we hear today is you can make it. You - it's always the you, you, you. It's always pointing to the man or to the lady. You can make it. God is with you.

I sat and heard a very famous preacher not long ago. I forced myself to watch him. I forced myself, because I don't like watching that stuff. So, okay, I wanna listen to what this man has to say. It was a message of hope. It was a message that was needed if I was going through a lawsuit. If I was going through a divorce, I could use it. If I had some problem, I could use it. But it lacked a great foundation. (emphasis added) Not one time did he say, turn to Jesus. It was inspirational, motivational. It helped you feel good about yourself, yes, it did. But I thought to myself, if somebody was in prison that would not do him one thing. Fifty thousand Christians today in North Korea are in labor camps. That message doesn't work with them.

Two hundred and thirty nine million today in the world, Christian people, are under persecution. That message means nothing to them. God is with you. You can make it, you can make it, you can make it, and they are killing them. You see, so that message of hope today is taking over America. It's a feel-good message. It's a self-help message. It's not the Gospel message. Our children are gonna collapse when persecution hits. Because persecution is coming. As surely as I'm sitting here talking to you, persecution will come to the West. It's already come to many, many parts of the world.

There are many sermons and messages today. They are motivational but lack a great foundation. This is of great concern to me. We cannot afford a generation of preachers who are motivational speakers who don't carry the fire of the gospel. Motivational messages are not enough to confront the wicked forces of the enemy. Those suffering persecution must hold onto the Cross, not motivation. The emerging generation is at risk. Look at what Matthew 11 says:

"How can I account for this generation? The people have been like spoiled children whining to their parents, 'We wanted to skip rope, and you were always too tired; we wanted to talk, but you were always too busy.' John came fasting and they called him crazy. I came feasting and they called me a boozer, a friend of the misfits. Opinion polls don't count for much, do they? The proof of the pudding is in the eating." (Matthew 11:16-19 MSG)

These are the prophetic words of Jesus perfectly describing our current generation. He described them as spoiled children. They wanted a feel-good message, a Santa Claus God. They were not ready to suffer through anything.

From this perspective and narrative of the state of the times during Jesus' earthly existence, He moved into action. His divine assignment was to bring into manifestation a social, spiritual, cultural, and structural change. He had to shake the whole system up; he had to bring about sharp change in order to rescue the generation from itself, and it was in alignment with His Father's will to do so. He is calling us to do the same.

Beyond any shred of doubt, I am convinced that each generation must fight its own set of battles to keep the very foundations of the legacies left for us. We cannot yield to the voice of spoiled children, but we must help the next generation keep and build upon a solid foundation. The Abolitionist Crusader, Wendell Phillips said: "The price of liberty is eternal vigilance."

... it was needful for me to write unto you, and exhort you that ye should earnestly contend for the faith which was once delivered unto the saints. (Jude 1:3b KJV)

Many that have gone before us have fought to gain liberties we now enjoy. However, the maintenance of that liberty comes at a cost. That cost is called eternal vigilance. One cannot afford to sleep because they have been set free. There are forces, elements, and oppositions that will put up a fight to always take one back into slavery.

Sons and daughters must build on the legacy that has been bequeathed to them by their fathers. They should also identify and understand the challenges the forebears went through to build a godly legacy and heritage for the generation today. If not, what is happening in Europe, for example, churches that have existed for centuries being sold and turned into hotels and entertainment centers, will repeat itself. This is an error!

The current generation may see this as a good business deal but are blinded to the fact that something of eternal value that was passed down to them is now lost. Today in America and other places, we are seeing churches that are void of hope for the future. The next generation is absent. The remaining members in the church are all above the age of 50. No new converts are joining the church... In a few years, the church will shut its doors and turn into a relic of past glory. This will begin happening in other parts of the world if we do not wake up and secure the ancient paths. Also, businesses that parents worked hard for to pass on as a legacy to their children will vanish.

For us to see the ultimate blessing in bridging the gap, the younger generation must appreciate and fight for the foundations and ancient paths the older generation has already established.

Because of God's grace to me, I have laid the foundation like an expert builder. Now others are building on it. But whoever is building on this foundation must be very careful. 11 For no one can lay any foundation other than the one we already have—Jesus Christ. (1 Corinthians 3:10-11 KJV)

*(*Full interview is available on Website or Link) https://youtu.be/DEfym8S0ih4*

CHAPTER 3

The Ancient landmarks

> *"If you cannot see where you are going, ask someone who has been there before." — J Loren Norris.*

My conversation with Pastor Benny reveals that we cannot remove the ancient landmarks referred to in Proverbs 22:28. The emerging generation is on a journey, but we have already passed through many of the destinations they must travel to and visit along the way. As true fathers, mothers, leaders, and mentors, we should become acquainted with the ancient landmarks, as were the apostles. In order to bridge the gap, we must embrace our responsibility to help this generation along the way and guide them with wisdom from our experience.

The apostles exemplified sacrifice. We must prepare the emerging generation for sacrifice so they do not become prey to the wiles and traps of the devil, and we must preach the authentic gospel and hold on to the faith for which the fathers contended. The word of God says in Proverbs 22:28, "The previous generation has set boundaries in place. Don't you dare move them just to benefit yourself." (The Passion Translation (TPT))

"Don't stealthily move back the boundary lines staked out long ago by your ancestors." (MSG)

"Remove not the ancient landmark, which thy fathers have set." (KJV)

Ancient Landmarks

For the sake of shared understanding across generations, it is important to list some of these landmarks. Examples of ancient of landmarks include:

- Sacrifice
- Loyalty
- Honor
- Process (and being Proven)
- Humility
- Remembrance

Let's explore each of these in more detail.

Sacrifice

And it came to pass after these things, that God did
tempt Abraham, and said unto him, Abraham: and he
said, Behold, here I am. 2 And he said, Take now thy
son, thine only son Isaac, whom thou lovest, and get
thee into the land of Moriah; and offer him there for
a burnt offering upon one of the mountains which I
will tell thee of. 3 And Abraham rose up early in the
morning, and saddled his ass, and took two of his
young men with him, and Isaac his son, and clave the
wood for the burnt offering, and rose up, and went
unto the place of which God had told him. 4 Then on
the third day Abraham lifted up his eyes, and saw the
place afar off. 5 And Abraham said unto his young
men, Abide ye here with the ass; and I and the lad
will go yonder and worship, and come again to you.
6 And Abraham took the wood of the burnt offering,
and laid it upon Isaac his son; and he took the fire
in his hand, and a knife; and they went both of them
together. 7 And Isaac spake unto Abraham his father,
and said, My father: and he said, Here am I, my son.
And he said, Behold the fire and the wood: but where
is the lamb for a burnt offering? 8 And Abraham said,
My son, God will provide himself a lamb for a burnt
offering: so they went both of them together. 9 And
they came to the place which God had told him of;

and Abraham built an altar there, and laid the wood in order, and bound Isaac his son, and laid him on the altar upon the wood. 10 And Abraham stretched forth his hand, and took the knife to slay his son. 11 And the angel of the Lord called unto him out of heaven, and said, Abraham, Abraham: and he said, Here am I. 12 And he said, Lay not thine hand upon the lad, neither do thou any thing unto him: for now I know that thou fearest God, seeing thou hast not withheld thy son, thine only son from me. (Genesis 22: 1-12 KJV)

Abraham's decision to sacrifice his son was a type and shadow of God Himself, offering His only Son for the sin of the world.

When I was born again, I used to walk five or six miles on foot to church to go worship and pray. I served my pastor, doing menial tasks to alleviate pressure from him, and I did it with joy. Without a heart of sacrifice, it would be difficult to walk away from careers to enter vocational/full-time ministry, put someone else's needs before our own. Jesus expects us to pick up our personal crosses and deny ourselves daily, which takes sacrifice.

Then said Jesus unto his disciples, If any man will come after me, let him deny himself, and take up his cross, and follow me. (Matthew 16:24 KJV)

In every generation, there are people who sacrifice their own needs, ambitions, and personal dreams to give themselves to a cause greater than themselves. By doing so, they become great, not by the world's standards, but by the kingdom's standards.

In the kingdom of God, whoever serves and sacrifices for others becomes great. We must be willing to sacrifice our ambition, time, titles, and talents. We cannot be a "what about me" generation. We

must be willing to lay our "Isaacs" on the altar. Abraham could have had a sense of entitlement, thinking to himself, "I've believed God all these years for this promised child. I went through Sarah nagging me about Hagar and had to send my other son away. I'm not sacrificing Isaac; I deserve to enjoy my son." He didn't think that way. He walked in obedience and was willing to sacrifice the thing that was most precious to him.

There's no room for a sense of entitlement because, like Abraham, each of us will be tested with sacrifice. Once you are tested and pass the test, you gain a greater appreciation for others who have gone before you and passed even greater tests. In every generation, we must go the way of sacrifice. It is an ancient landmark every generation must embrace to bridge the gap.

Loyalty

Loyalty is a faithful adherence to an individual, leader, nation, or organization, vision or mission. To adhere means to stick to something or with someone.

Ruth demonstrates great and fierce loyalty when she says to Naomi, her mother-in-law, "Don't urge me to leave you or to turn back from you. Where you go I will go, and where you stay I will stay. Your people will be my people and your God my God." (Ruth 1:15-16) She made a commitment to stick with Naomi without any hope of finding a bright future.

Naomi and Ruth are two phenomenal women who model the great characters of loyalty, acceptance, and kindness towards each other. They both suffered overwhelming mutual grief and loss.

Much like the poor, frightened, and desperate people trying to get out of Afghanistan, Ukraine, or any calamity-stricken area, Naomi, and her husband, Elimelech, and their two sons, Mahlon and Chilion, made the risky decision to flee their home country in the hope of finding a better life and future for their family.

Naomi and her family leave Bethlehem, which is five miles south of Jerusalem and travel perhaps some twenty to thirty miles or more east of the Dead Sea and south of the river Arnon to the land of Moab.

The Israelites believed that the Moabites were related to them through the nephew of Abraham, called Lot (Genesis 19:37), but because the Moabites didn't give the Israelites food and water on their journey out of Egypt, it says in Deuteronomy 23:23 that, "No Moabite shall be admitted to the assembly of the Lord," and there were hard feelings for generations. Yet this is where Naomi's family chose to go. There was no closer option than Moab. Pride, status, or class wasn't going to stop them from doing something about their deteriorating condition.

The situation for Naomi's family grows much more serious when her husband dies leaving her and their two sons even more vulnerable. Then both of the young men married Moabite women. But sadly, after they had lived in Moab about ten years, both of Naomi's sons died leaving their wives as widows and their mother childless, in addition to having no husband.

It is hard to imagine what it must feel like to be living in an unfamiliar country, lose so many members of one's family, and feel alone and unsupported with nowhere to turn for help. Naomi, who was from an older generation, played such a unique role in the life of Ruth, who was younger. Ruth resolved in her heart never to leave Naomi, despite her pain, grief, and loss when her husband died. Imagine what the life and state of Ruth would have been without the love, kindness, mentorship, strength, and courage she derived from Naomi.

Likewise, Naomi had lost her husband and both of her sons. She had to cope with her sense of grief and loss to figure out what she would do and how she would survive. In Ruth 1:21 she said, "I went out full, but the LORD has brought me back empty. Why do you call me Naomi, since the LORD has witnessed against me and the Almighty has afflicted me?" But in actual fact she was not going back empty, because she had Ruth.

We demonstrate loyalty when we can stick with our leaders, fathers, and mothers in their difficult times and not be ashamed of their scars. Everyone wants to stay when things are good, but when we stick with them through challenging times, we demonstrate loyalty. Each generation must stick with the other through good and bad. We cannot be ashamed to identify with one another. Jesus said, "I and my father are one." Loyalty is also an ancient landmark every generation must embrace to bridge the gap.

Honor

"No," Jesus said, "I have no demon in me. For I honor my Father—and you dishonor me.

(John 8:49 NLT)

To honor means to prize, value, esteem, pay homage to, revere, or respect. Honor means treating someone with respect because you value them. Romans 13:7 (ERV) says, "Give everyone what you owe them. If you owe them any kind of tax, then pay it. Show respect to those you should respect. And show honor to those you should honor." Then, 1 Timothy 5:17 (KJV) tells us, "Let the elders that rule well be counted worthy of double honour, especially they who labour in the word and doctrine." So it is clear that those who labor in the ministry should be honored, not because we like or dislike them, but because of their labor. There must be honor for the labor and for the responsibility of the office, whether we think the person deserves it or not. We must come to the place where we can appreciate the labor of the generations that preceded us, for we build upon their labor.

We must also understand that honor works by the law of reciprocity. If you dishonor someone who should be honored, you attract dishonor. If you honor those who should be honored, you attract honor. God said it this way in 1 Samuel 2:30 KJV, "for them that honour me I will honour, and they that despise me shall be lightly esteemed." God is letting us know that honor works by the law of reciprocity. If you sow honor, you will reap it back. If you sow dishonor, you will reap light esteem (dishonor) back.

It is also important to know that honor should be from the heart. In Isaiah 29:13 KJV, God said, "Forasmuch as this people draw near me with their mouth, and with their lips do honour me, but have removed their heart far from me." There is a difference between lip service and someone truly being important to you. Look at this Scripture again:

The Lord says, "These people come to honor me with words, but I am not really important to them. The worship they give me is nothing but human rules they have memorized. (Isaiah 29:13 ERV)

To honor a father or mother from the heart brings great blessing. It attracts honor back to you and brings long life. Let us genuinely honor from the heart to unlock the associated blessings. Honor is associated with one of the Ten Commandments and is an ancient landmark to bridge the gap. Every generation must take hold of it.

To ram home the thoughts on honor, there's a story in the Bible with very poignant principles that all must know. A prophetic declaration had been made about Elisha the son of Shaphat to succeed a discarded Elijah. He was to be a prophet in the stead of Elijah. He subsequently crossed the Jordan river with Elijah and did receive a mantle and a double portion of his spirit. Then comes the intriguing part of the whole saga of anointing. At the river in the application of the mantle upon the water Elisha calls upon the God of Elijah instead of his God who was the same. The river opened and gave him dry ground to cross because he called upon the God of his father. Inability to honor can maim the young and for sure there are many young ones who are stuck in their places of transition not because they are not gifted or carry mantles but the dishonor of the old has denied them total access to the breakthroughs available.

Processed/Proven

Everything in God is progressive. We go from faith to faith, and from glory to glory. God takes us through processes to work in us and through us, and to work out of us anything that needs to be driven out for him to be glorified in our lives. A faith that has not been tested cannot be trusted. Many do not want testing and trying, but it is the way of the Lord. He prunes us so we can bear greater fruit.

David went through major processes. While all his brothers were in the house, he was in the fields with the sheep. And even after he was anointed, there was a time of processing. He didn't immediately ascend to the throne after the oil was poured on his head. Some ministers think that the oil is all it takes, but that is mistaken thinking. Longevity does not come from the oil; it comes from going through the processes and dealings of God to develop character.

David's processes allowed him a point of reference. When the time came for him to confront the biggest challenge of his life, he could refer to his process. He could say, "When I kept my father's sheep, the lion and the bear came, and I slew them." If he had not gone through his process in the wilderness, he would not have been prepared to face Goliath. Process builds confidence, faith, and a point of reference in times of trouble; it makes you 'battle ready' and empowers you to withstand the pressures of leadership. Process builds experiential knowledge and wisdom.

David served Saul, who he had been anointed to replace. Can you imagine how some preachers today would have handled this? They are anointed yet being asked to serve the one they are anointed to replace. Many would not have the character or patience to endure it. Yet David served Saul, playing anointed music skillfully for him, and in the process bringing deliverance, he saw demons leave Saul. But continued to honor Saul from his heart.

David endured long battles, but he "waxed stronger and stronger." He wasn't just anointed, he had character, endurance, and perseverance, which only comes from serving and being processed.

Now there was long war between the house of Saul and the house of David: but David waxed stronger and stronger, and the house of Saul waxed weaker and weaker. (2 Samuel 3:1 KJV)

Strength and stamina are developed through process. 1 Timothy 3:6 says, "Not a novice, lest being lifted up with pride he fall into the condemnation of the devil." Processing and proving is another ancient landmark every generation must embrace to bridge the gap.

Humility

In the same way, you who are younger, submit yourselves to your elders. All of you, clothe yourselves with humility toward one another, because, "God opposes the proud but shows favor to the humble." 6 Humble yourselves, therefore, under God's mighty hand, that he may lift you up in due time. (1 Peter 5:5-6 NIV)

Humility is a state of being and an attitude of the heart. It means having a right understanding of one's state as a created thing and bringing yourself under the Lordship and mastership of Jesus Christ. Humility also has to do with being modest, in the sense of having a modest opinion or estimate of one's own importance, rank, or station in life. 1 Peter 5:5 instructs the younger generation to submit to the older. This involves coming under the older. The prefix "sub-" means under. To submit to the older, the younger generation must come under. They must humble themselves to come under the guidance and wisdom of the elders. They must come down in their attitude of heart and estimation of their own importance. Paul admonishes us in Romans 12:3 NIV, saying, "...Do not think of yourself more highly than you ought, but rather think of yourself with sober judgment, in accordance with the faith God has distributed to each of you. (Romans 12:3b NIV)

Similarly, the older generation must walk in humility. 1 Peter 5:5 also says, "All of you, clothe yourselves with humility toward one another." It then goes on to sound an alert declaring, "God opposes the proud but shows favor to the humble." God actively resists the proud person or generation. The elders must also walk in humility; they must not think they are above apologizing or saying, "I'm sorry." We must be humble enough to recognize that we need to work with the younger generation and accept them when they make mistakes. We must all walk in humility, and our greatest example of humility is Jesus.

"and being found in fashion as a man, he humbled himself, and became obedient unto death, even the death of the cross."

Philippians 2:8 KJV

We must willingly humble ourselves and follow the example of Christ, remembering James 4:10 which says, "Humble yourselves in the sight of the Lord, and he shall lift you up."

There is the need to say here that humility is not an expression of the mouth nor little acts done here and there. It is an attitude that finds expression in every sphere of human activity. One thing that all should know is, humility will be tested at various junctions of our walk with God.

Peter, a very outspoken disciple of Jesus remonstrated with Jesus and told him there was no need to go to die as Jesus intimated. The rebuke Peter got for a good intention of care albeit demonic influence was very sharp. "Get thee behind me Satan for you savorest not the things of God but rather men" an intention of care got this sharp rebuke from Jesus. Now comes the journey Peter had to walk. The pathway of humility to accept this open rebuke in the presence of all and take it in good faith without offense. For sure a lot will be offended because this rebuke stings the face of pride and will bring much anguish to every proud heart. Remember pride is the exact opposite of humility.

Humility is an ancient landmark that every generation must take hold of in order to bridge the gap.

Gratitude/Remembrance

The famous deaf educator, Jean Baptiste Massieu, made a statement that is now considered a French proverb: "Gratitude is the memory of the heart."

Indeed, appreciation comes when you feel grateful from the depths of your heart. The head keeps an account of all the benefits you give and receive, but the heart records the appreciation, humility, and generosity that one feels when someone showers you with kindness.

"When thou hast eaten and art full, then thou shalt bless the LORD thy God for the good land which he hath given thee. Beware that thou forget not the LORD thy God, in not keeping his commandments, and his judgments, and his statutes, which I command thee this day: lest when thou hast eaten and art full, and hast built goodly houses, and dwelt therein; and when thy herds and thy flocks multiply, and thy silver and thy gold is multiplied, and all that thou hast is multiplied; then thine heart be lifted up, and thou forget the LORD thy God, which brought thee forth out of the land of Egypt, from the house of bondage; who led thee through that great and terrible wilderness, wherein were fiery serpents, and scorpions, and drought, where there was no water; who brought thee forth water out of the rock of flint;"

> *"When thou hast eaten and art full, then thou shalt bless the LORD thy God for the good land which he hath given thee. Beware that thou forget not the LORD thy God, in not keeping his commandments, and his judgments, and his statutes, which I command thee this day: lest when thou hast eaten and art full, and hast built goodly houses, and dwelt therein; and when thy herds and thy flocks multiply, and thy silver and thy gold is multiplied, and all that thou hast is multiplied; then thine heart be lifted up, and thou forget the LORD thy God, which brought thee forth out of the land of Egypt, from the house of bondage; who led thee through that great and terrible wilderness, wherein were fiery serpents, and scorpions, and drought, where there was no water; who brought thee forth water out of the rock of flint; who fed thee in the wilderness with manna, which thy fathers knew not, that he might humble thee, and that he might prove thee, to do thee good at thy latter end; and thou say in thine heart, My power and the might of*

mine hand hath gotten me this wealth. But thou shalt remember the LORD thy God: for it is he that giveth thee power to get wealth, that he may establish his covenant which he sware unto thy fathers, as it is this day. And it shall be, if thou do at all forget the LORD thy God, and walk after other gods, and serve them, and worship them, I testify against you this day that ye shall surely perish. As the nations which the LORD destroyeth before your face, so shall ye perish; because ye would not be obedient unto the voice of the LORD your God."

Deuteronomy 8:10 -20 KJV

God, in his graciousness and love, gently nudges us on the need to place a premium on remembrance and the expression of gratitude. I have always said that an attitude of gratitude is always a seed for more. Whenever we remember the good done to us and take intentional steps to express gratitude towards our benefactors, we open ourselves up to endless and immeasurable possibilities of blessings and opportunities from the heavens above, as well as humanity.

The possibility of forgetting, after you are full and not wanting or lacking anything materially, is very high. Our hearts become puffed up and we attribute the success and breakthroughs to our own strength.

This, unfortunately, is something that has plagued both generations, old and young alike.

Young people have never been old before, but every old person today was once a young person. It is, therefore, necessary for the old generation to make it a point, as part of bridging the gap, to consciously teach and guide the younger generation how to value, practice and uphold the deep spiritual values of remembrance and gratitude.

Ecclesiastes 12:1 says, "Remember your Creator in the days of your youth, before the days of trouble come and the years approach when you will say, "I find no pleasure in them."

God wants the young generation to enjoy their youth, as well as their old age. We are reminded of what we must do while young, in order to bridge the gap for a successful and fruitful old age. It is called remembrance. When you are mindful and remember, you do things according to the will of God. I strive daily to say thank you for small favors people go out of their way to do for me. I believe if I am faithful in little, I will also be faithful in much. Gratitude and remembering are important ancient landmarks every generation must embrace, to bridge the gap.

Maintaining the Landmarks

These important landmarks are essential to bridging the gap between generations. However, the ability to maintain them depends on a few very important ideas.

1. Knowledge: The Scripture says, "My people are destroyed for lack of knowledge." Being knowledgeable of how these landmarks were established, specifically, the experiences of the patriarchs and matriarchs in Scripture, is vital. Acquiring knowledge about their experience in Scripture empowers us to gain the wisdom necessary to maintain the landmarks. The same obedience and faith it take to establish a landmark will be needed to maintain it.

2. Obedience: We must be obedient to practice the time-honored principles and values of the Scriptures embedded in the ancient landmarks we've highlighted thus far. Obedience is better than sacrifice.

3. Intentional Effort: Each generation must consciously and intentionally work to make sure these ancient landmarks are maintained.

If each generation would commit to adhering to these landmarks and use them as a starting point for understanding and bridge building, the gaps between us would diminish at a faster pace. However, maintaining the landmarks does not come automatically or at no cost.

They can be maintained and improved upon only when we are eternally vigilant through intentional processes to preserve what was left to us by the previous generation. We should build upon them, or at the very least, preserve them for the generations that will come after us. We must not destroy or diminish them. Each generation must pay the price to do so for the sake of another. No generation can get to its appointed destination by bypassing the ancient landmarks. We must all go the way of sacrifice, loyalty, honor, gratitude, humility, and process. Skipping these destination stops means skipping an essential part of character development, which ultimately jeopardizes the future.

CHAPTER 4

Modeling Honor

For though ye have ten thousand instructors in Christ, yet have ye not many fathers: for in Jesus Christ, I have begotten you through the gospel.

(1 Corinthians 4:15 KJV)

I firmly believe that transparency and authenticity are important attributes of transformational leadership. Through our successes, failures, and shortcomings we ourselves and others can also learn and be better. It is also a key component in bridging the gap with the generations looking up to us to see that we are not perfect, we make mistakes, we miss it sometimes, but we learn from the mistakes and move forward.

I am not ashamed to tell the story of where the Lord picked me up from and some of the valuable lessons I have learned along the way. One such lesson was how to honor my fathers, first spiritual and then natural.

I was privileged to be fathered by very powerful and exceptional leaders. I was a mess when my journey started...I saw these powerful men and never thought of attaining the heights they had ascended, but God in his infinite wisdom placed them in my path for my growth and development, and the fulfillment of his purpose for my life. I recognize that fatherhood is not just a title, but also learned behavior that must be modeled for people to see, imitate, and follow.

My spiritual father, Archbishop Benson Idahosa of blessed memory, was a very great and powerful man. He was truly a giant in the Kingdom of God, and I learned a valuable lesson about honor and the role it plays in bridging the gap. When Oral Roberts and Archbishop Benson Idahosa came to have a crusade in Ghana, it was publicized in Oral's magazine that Idahosa's Church in Ghana was hosting it, even though my church was hosting the event. I was ill-advised by a young man, who was working closely with me, to respond to the misprint and not just leave it alone. I responded by writing a letter to Oral Roberts to explain that it was my church and not Idahosa's church hosting the crusade. Oral Roberts forwarded the letter I wrote to him to Idahosa and said, "This is what your son sent to me." So Idahosa sent a delegation with a letter to me in Ghana and asked me to come see him so we can resolve the issue. I told the delegation I was not coming.

They asked me, "Nicholas, do you know what you are doing?" I said, "Yes, I am not coming." So they left and after they left, I received a letter from my father, Archbishop Benson Idahosa that said, "Now that you have come of age and everything, you are on your own." I prayed and made declarations, tore the letter, burnt it, and went about my business.

After that, all hell broke loose! For two years, I was under investigation, all kinds of attacks, interrogations, threatening, assassination attempts, and media attacks. It was about two years of buffeting and ceaseless attacks. Even though I was fasting and having all night prayer meetings for that entire duration, nothing was changing.

So I reached out to the man who taught me how to pray, my elder from the Church of Pentecost, and shared with him what was going on. He said to me,

"I will talk to the Lord and get back to you and let you know what he will say to you." After a couple of days, he called me and said, "The reason for what is going on is because," the Lord said, "You have touched one of his anointed and until you fix it and resolve the issue, [the attacks] are not going to stop." So, I did everything to reach my spiritual father, but I couldn't get to him. When I finally saw him in London, I fell on my face, held his leg, and cried out "mercy". I apologized to him, and he forgave me and prayed for me. And this is the prayer he said, "Satan, this is between me and my son, stay out of it" After that the attacks came to an end.

I found out later an interesting revelation from one of the operatives of the then Bureau of National Investigation(BNI), now NIB, who confided in me. He told me that for over a long period of time they had tried on several occasions been instructed to pick me up but something always occurred to disrupt their mission for the day. Interestingly, they succeeded in picking me up just around the time my spiritual father and I had the issue, per my calculations.

I learnt a very valuable lesson about honor. It delivers us from the enemy's onslaught and preserves us from being prematurely destroyed.

"He that diggeth a pit shall fall into it; and whoso breaketh an hedge, a serpent shall bite him."

Ecclesiastes 10 :8 KJV

Whatever it takes, it is worth honoring your spiritual father. He may not have a church like yours but keep honoring him because the more you honor him, the more you will be honored. And never believe that you are greater than he is because you have a big church. Having a big church does not make you a father, neither do large numbers. Being a father is a calling. It is an appointment and an ordination. You did not decide who your father and mother would be. Therefore, your spiritual father is your father for a reason. Respect and honor him, and it will go well with you.

I have a lot of sons and daughters all over the world. Those who are doing very well are those who serve faithfully and bless me financially and in many other ways. Those who fail to honor me, may be anointed, but they are in distress. The Bible says, "Whatever you sow, you will reap."

If you sow honor, you will reap honor. Bless your spiritual fathers and mothers. It is a key that will take you far. Whenever I am going through crises and difficult times, I look for some minister—a man or woman—years ahead of me in ministry, to bless financially. As soon as I do that, a shift occurs and something happens that favors me.

The same is true for biological fathers. I implore every son and daughter to bless your natural father and mother, so it will be well with you.

My biological father was a very powerful man. He was a chief, diplomat, statesman, and politician, amongst other things. He was a difficult man to please, but I vowed that I would do everything in my power to honor him. I realized that every one of my siblings who had problems with him and dishonored him, had serious issues and difficulties.

One of my brothers, Kwamena, had problems with my dad and would always try to stand up to him or fight him. I remember speaking with him to encourage making peace with the old man, but he refused. He kept insisting on standing his ground and resisting and opposing him. Before I left Ghana for London, I spoke with him, once more, to make peace, but he did not. When I arrived in London, I received a message that he had died. He had fallen, with blood coming from his nose, between my Dad's door and his room. When my dad heard about what happened he said, "He is a cursed son, take him from the morgue and bury him. Do not bring him to my house." It was very sad!

The Lord really helped me to honor my natural father and spiritual fathers. I stood with and served their vision, mandate, and ministry in any way I could, by flying to visit, support, and pray with them, and sow into their vision, family, and staff. I hosted some of them in Ghana. I always blessed them when they came to bless the nation and God's people. It wasn't easy, because it really stretched me and my family physically, financially, and emotionally in many ways.

However, the relationship was more important, and sometimes required going above and beyond, giving it my best and all, but it was worth it. The blessings and impartations I received from them as well as being adopted as a son and gleaning from them is what has made me the father I am today. My prayer is that I am able to be for my sons and daughters what my spiritual fathers were for me. Hopefully, my sons and daughters will pass it on to the generations after them, so that they are stronger and more powerful, in Jesus' mighty name!

CHAPTER 5

Heart of the Father

"Behold, I will send you Elijah the prophet before the coming of the great and dreadful day of the Lord: And he shall turn the heart of the fathers to the children, and the heart of the children to their fathers, lest I come and smite the earth with a curse."

Malachi 4: 5-6

The prophet in closing the Old Testament, said, God will turn the hearts of the fathers to the sons, and the hearts of the sons to the fathers, lest there be a gap that will attract a curse, because God hates gaps (voids).

Bridging the gap is a very serious subject. The enemy has succeeded to put a wedge between the old generation and the new generation through misunderstanding. It is the responsibility of the fathering generation to remove this gap and teach and train the next generation.

Take a look in scripture at Mary representing the young generation, and Elizabeth, representing the old generation. They were both pregnant at the same time and God orchestrated the timing for them to need one another. They couldn't do without each other. This gives us a glimpse of the need for the old (those further along in age) and the young (those just starting out) to work together through similar issues. The baby that Elizabeth was carrying, John the Baptist, was assigned to be the forerunner of the baby that Mary was carrying, the Lord Jesus. The Lord Jesus was greater than John the Baptist, but He humbled Himself to be baptized by what the old generation had carried. As we bridge the gap between the old and the emerging generations, we will need understanding and humility. We need humility, because without humility we end up working in partnership with the adversary against God. James 4:6 says, "...God resist the proud, but giveth grace to the humble."

Jesus came to reconcile man back to the Father. A gap was created through sin. Jesus then became the bridge, and connector to reconcile man back to the Father by his death. That finished work gave all of us who believe, access to the presence of God. Jesus humbled himself to the point of death. Humility then, should become our posture- not a mentality or attitude of entitlement.

By God's grace, He has given me the opportunity to train and raise sons and daughters in ministry. At a point in my life, I started having problems with some of the sons I brought up in ministry. Many are financially well off. These are sons that I have laid hands on and prayed for. I do not have a private jet, but some of them do. Then the Lord began to deal with my heart. He said, "Son, it's to your glory and your honour for them to do well. Don't be upset with them, pray for them. Pray against the veil. Pray against pride and arrogance." So, I started dealing with my heart, because I realized that, based on their works, some of them were trying to be in my position. Some of them seemed to want to become my father, telling me what I should do.

Among the bishops I brought up, one was doing so well. So well, that he stopped calling me Papa. He would call me Archbishop. Anytime he was in trouble then he would call and say "Papa," and I would say,

"Who is this?" He would say, "Your son." And I would ask, " Which of my sons?" He said, "Papa, you don't know your son's voice?" And I said, "Oh, I thought I'm Archbishop, I didn't know I was Papa." He had become so successful, so big, that he wanted to become my father. But you must watch your heart; because if you are not careful, you will kill your own son.

I think of David and his relationship with Saul. If David went with Saul to the battlefield instead of Jonathan, Saul wouldn't have died, because David would have protected him. But you know what the devil did? The devil provoked Saul with envy against his own son and made Saul go after his son David and drove him out into the wilderness. There were multiple assassination attempts on David's life by King Saul. And because of that, he remained isolated. The strength of David that could have preserved him was not there, so he died prematurely.

Hear my heart, existing generation. If we don't guide and guard ourselves; in the day of need, we will not have anybody to fight for us. Do you know what the enemy is doing? He is killing both the old and young generations prematurely.

> *"And it came to pass, that, when Jesus was returned, the people gladly received him: for*

they were all waiting for him. And, behold, there came a man named Jairus, and he was a ruler of the synagogue: and he fell down at Jesus' feet, and besought him that he would come into his house: for he had one only daughter, about twelve years of age, and she lay a dying. But as he went the people thronged him. And a woman having an issue of blood twelve years, which had spent all her living upon physicians, neither could be healed of any, came behind him, and touched the border of his garment: and immediately her issue of blood stanched. And Jesus said, Who touched me? When all denied, Peter and they that were with him said, Master, the multitude throng thee and press thee, and sayest thou, Who touched me? And Jesus said, Somebody hath touched me: for I perceive that virtue is gone out of me. And when the woman saw that she was not hid, she came trembling, and falling down before him, she declared unto him before all the people for what cause she had touched him, and how she was healed immediately. And he said unto her, Daughter, be of good comfort: thy faith hath made thee whole; go in peace. While he yet spake, there cometh one from the ruler of the synagogue's house, saying to him, Thy daughter is dead: trouble not the Master. But when Jesus heard it, he answered him, saying, Fear not: believe only, and she shall be made whole. And when

> *he came into the house, he suffered no man to go in, save Peter, and James, and John, and the father and the mother of the maiden. And all wept, and bewailed her: but he said, Weep not; she is not dead, but sleepeth. And they laughed him to scorn, knowing that she was dead. And he put them all out, and took her by the hand, and called, saying, Maid, arise. And her spirit came again, and she arose straightway: and he commanded to give her meat."*
>
> *Luke 8 :40 -55 KJV*

Okay

We see the story of Jairus' daughter who was sick at the age of twelve years and dying. At the same time as Jesus was going to heal the young girl, the woman suffering from an issue of blood for twelve years, pressed her way to touch the hem of Jesus' garment, and gained her healing. Jairus' daughter died at the age of twelve, the woman suffering from an issue of blood suffered for twelve years. The devil killed the twelve-year-old and tried for twelve years to kill the old generation as well.

I yearn expectantly that the old generation will bless the young generation. However, in order to do so, the older generation must deal with the issues that are causing them to bleed, so that they can receive the healing they need. This will result in them having the strength to help the younger generation gain healing as well.

The way Jesus fathered His disciples was unique. He took more time in training leaders than He did ministering to the multitude. He took time to answer questions, deal with motives of the heart and attitudes, and taught them how to relate to one another and do ministry by allowing them to do it themselves. He evaluated what was done and gave feedback and corrections.

You do not need a megachurch to be a father or mother to the young generation. You do not have to have a private jet to be a father. It is simply taking time to mentor, train and nurture the emerging generation by first exemplifying the love and acceptance of the Heavenly Father to them. Spiritual fatherhood and motherhood is an ordination and an office. My father or mother will always be my father and my mother no matter how big and huge I become.

Passing the torch...

> *"And the things that thou hast heard of me among many witnesses, the same commit thou to faithful men, who shall be able to teach others also."*
>
> *2 Timothy 2:2 KJV*

Consider this carefully, Moses had a spiritual son called Joshua. However, Joshua was a son and not a father. Where is Joshua's son? Who took Joshua's mantle? There are no records in scripture that Joshua fathered anyone or passed the mantle to anyone. It is easy to be a son, but being a father is very different.

Let's look at another scenario. Elijah had a son called Elisha. Elisha was a son. Elisha had no son. Where is his son? He went to the grave with his mantle. He performed more miracles than his father, but because the one he should have raised as a son, failed at making himself available to be mentored by his father and to be raised as a son, he could not pass on his mantle. Instead, Elisha cursed him because of greed.

I am not condoning his actions, but, a true father with a heart for the next generation does not curse his only child. Being a father is not easy.

David was such a trans-generational thinker that he secured everything Solomon needed for the temple to make sure he succeeded in his biggest assignment, to build a temple for the Lord.

> *"And David commanded to gather together the strangers that were in the land of Israel; and he set masons to hew wrought stones to build the house of God. And David prepared*

iron in abundance for the nails for the doors of the gates, and for the joinings; and brass in abundance without weight; also cedar trees in abundance: for the Zidonians and they of Tyre brought much cedar wood to David. And David said, Solomon my son is young and tender, and the house that is to be builded for the LORD must be exceeding magnifical, of fame and of glory throughout all countries: I will therefore now make preparation for it. So David prepared abundantly before his death. Then he called for Solomon his son, and charged him to build an house for the LORD God of Israel. And David said to Solomon, My son, as for me, it was in my mind to build an house unto the name of the LORD my God: but the word of the LORD came to me, saying, Thou hast shed blood abundantly, and hast made great wars: thou shalt not build an house unto my name, because thou hast shed much blood upon the earth in my sight."

1 Chronicles 22 :2 -8 KJV

"O LORD our God, all this store that we have prepared to build thee an house for thine holy name cometh of thine hand, and is all thine own. I know also, my God, that thou triest the heart, and hast pleasure in uprightness. As for me, in the uprightness of mine heart I have willingly offered all these things: and now have I seen with joy thy people, which are present here, to

offer willingly unto thee."

1 Chronicles 29 :16 -17 KJV

Here are a few lessons from David for the fathering generation:

1. He prayed transgenerational prayers for his son Solomon 1Chronicles 29:19 "And give Solomon my son a perfect heart, to keep thy commandments, thy testimonies, and thy statues, and to do all these things, and to build the palace, for the which I have made provision."

2. He ensured a peaceful transfer of power. 1 Chronicles 29:22, "...and they made Solomon the son of David king the second time and anointed him into the Lord to be the chief governor, and Zadok to be priest. Then Solomon sat on the throne of the Lord as king instead of David, his father, and prospered; and all Israel obeyed him."

3. He made sure all the people who helped him and served him pledged allegiance to Solomon. 1 Chronicles 29:24, "and all the princes, and the mighty men, and all the sons likewise of King David, submitted themselves likewise unto the king David, submitted themselves unto Solomon the king."

4. David fought to make sure every enemy was conquered so that Solomon would have peace to build because he didn't want him to fight unnecessary battles. 1 Kings 5:3-4, "Thou knowest that David my father was unable to build a house for the name of the LORD his God because of the wars which surrounded him, until the LORD put them under the soles of his feet. "But now the LORD my God has given me rest on every side; there is neither adversary nor misfortune."

5. He left such a legacy that it affected subsequent generations like Hezekiah, Asa, Jehosophat. They were all delivered because of their father David.

6. He served God and God could not ignore his generations, (Solomon, Rehoboam, etc.)

   1 Kings 11:12 "Then the LORD said to Solomon, "Because you have done this and have not kept My covenant and My statutes, which I have commanded you, I will tear the kingdom away from you and give it to your servant. Nevertheless, for the sake of your father David, I will not do it during your lifetime; I will tear it out of the hand of your son. Yet I will not tear the whole kingdom away from him. I will give one tribe to your son for the sake of My servant David and for the sake of Jerusalem, which I have chosen.

7. David served his generation Acts 13:36 "For David, after he had served his own generation by the will of God, fell on sleep, and was laid unto his fathers, and saw corruption."

The tragedy of leaving chaos behind, no plan of succession, selfishness, being power hungry to the extent that people are willing to die without grooming or refusing to teach anyone is quite troubling. This is not the way it should end for any father.

Transgenerational thinkers know and believe that success without a successor is no success. Therefore, they endeavor to do everything in their power to make sure that leadership or their work continues, whether it be in a family, politics, the church, in business, an empire, or in ministry. There must be clear lines of succession.

CHAPTER 6

The Rising Generation: Standing on Shoulders

Verily, verily, I say unto you, He that believeth on me, the works that I do shall he do also; and greater works than these shall he do; because I go unto my Father.

(John 14:12 KJV)

We have established that the fathering generation has a responsibility to train and mentor the emerging generation. But there is more to it than that. The emerging generation also has a responsibility to recognize that they will go farther by not disconnecting from the older generation, but rather, build on what the fathering generation offers.

Proper perspective is needed. When Jesus said, “Greater works than these shall he do,” it did not mean he would be greater than Jesus. In light of the following Scriptures, that could not have been what Jesus meant:

Verily, verily, I say unto you, The servant is not greater than his lord; neither he that is sent greater than he that sent him. (John 13:16 KJV)

Remember the word that I said unto you, The servant is not greater than his lord. If they have persecuted me, they will also persecute you; if they have kept my saying, they will keep yours also. (John 15:20 KJV)

According to John 13:16, no one is greater than the one that sent him. Parents send their children like arrows, and children who do not allow themselves to be sent think they are “greater” than their parents, do well and walk in wisdom. Some feel they have arrived, and therefore, do not have to honor their parents or elders. This is not the heart of a son reflected in the Scriptures.

There are some cultures who demonstrate this principle better than others. In some cultures, it is common for children to take care of their parents in their older years. You will observe three generations living together under one roof, with children seeing their parents honoring and taking care of their grandparents. For example, there is an African proverb which says, "When a child knows how to wash his hands well, he eats with the elders." This simply means if you do not lose respect for the older generation, you will become great yourself.

Jesus said greater works shall you do than me. This means, based on the knowledge available from the exploits, failures, and successes of the old generation, the young generation is able to execute better, faster, and greater. But greater works does not make you greater than your father or mother. Greater works does not mean you are greater than those who sent you.

Take Elisha and Elijah. Elijah performed seven miracles. Elisha performed fourteen miracles. Does that mean Elisha is greater than Elijah? Elisha performed fourteen miracles because he was carrying his father's mantle. The father performed seven, the son performed fourteen. Yet, on the Mount of Transfiguration when Jesus was transformed, it was not Elisha that was talking to Jesus—it was Elijah the father.

Also, consider Joshua and Moses. Joshua successfully took the people of Israel into the promised land. Moses didn't enter the promised land physically. Does that mean that Joshua is greater than Moses? Yet, on the Mount of Transfiguration when Jesus was transformed, it was not Joshua that was talking to Jesus—it was Moses the father.

The generations must critically evaluate how they define success. Elijah and Elisha show us that you cannot define success by numbers. The values of the day may not reflect the values embedded in the ancient landmarks. If the generations (old and emerging) evaluate one another from the values of the day, they will lose respect for one another and not work together the way God intended. So how do you define success? If we are not careful, we will misplace our priorities and be misguided by pride.

We need to value the wisdom available to us no matter how successful or unsuccessful the world labels our fathers, mothers, mentors, and leaders. We need to learn how to stand on the shoulders of their experiences, wisdom, faith, perseverance, and insight.

Rise Higher: Stand on My Shoulders

> *"There is no such thing as a self-made man. You will reach your goals only with the help of others." – George Shinn*

We should appreciate technological innovations that make life easier for us. However, we should also realize that each technological innovation builds from former technology. Without a VCR, there would not have been a DVD player, and without a DVD player, there would have not been blu-ray, mp3, and so on. Even scientists and engineers are smart enough to research the technologies that exist before they embark on new innovations.

This generation has the most wonderful and the greatest of opportunities to stand on the shoulders of the fathers that have gone ahead so they can see beyond their days. You do not have to be in ministry for forty-five years like me to have what I have. It is pride, arrogance, ignorance, and a waste of everyone's time when you try to reinvent the wheel. You can take it from here—where I am and have arrived, and run with it to the next level.

I strongly desire to impress this upon you as you read this book, because a lot of things disturb me about this generation, the young, up and coming generation, and the old generation. It will take understanding to bridge the gap. It will take humility for us to stay connected to each other and not allow gaps to divide us.

Stay connected: Do Not Go Alone

In the same way, you who are younger must accept the authority of the elders. And all of you, dress yourselves in humility as you relate to one another, for "God opposes the proud but gives grace to the humble." 6 So humble yourselves under the mighty power of God, and at the right time he will lift you up in honor. (1 Peter 5:5-6 NLT)

Coming together is a beginning.

Staying together is progress.

Working together is a success.

Humility builds a bridge between it all.

Once we come together, we must stay together. After we stay together, we must work together. Humility is necessary to do all of these—coming together, keeping together, and working together—because we cannot afford to go alone. No one is an island to himself or herself.

Pharaoh had a dream that he did not understand, and it was troubling him night after night. The answer to his problem was in one from the younger generation, who had been processed and mantled by his father.

Joseph was a young man. Joel 2:28 says, "your old men shall dream dreams, your young men shall see visions." Still, Joseph was able to dream instead of seeing visions, because he carried his father's coat of many colors as well as his father's mantle. He was dreaming not because of his age, but because he carried his father's mantle. He could see through the father's mantle. So he didn't just see visions, he also dreamed dreams.

Whether it be his biological father's house, Potiphar's house, the prison, or the palace, in each place Joseph went, he served faithfully.

He served his father by running errands for him. He ran Potiphar's house and remained faithful, refusing to sin against him by touching his wife. He served the prison warden, and he served Pharoah. He stayed connected to whatever authority he found himself under. Joseph connected through service and honor.

Like Joseph, we must stay connected. We cannot afford to embrace a "lone ranger" mentality. Don't try to go alone, and don't let the enemy convince you that you are the only one trying to do what you are doing. That was Elijah's downfall. Remember, whatever you are doing, you are standing on the shoulders of someone else's sacrifice.

Removing "Lone Ranger Mentality"

> *"If you want to go fast, go alone, if you want to go far, go together." – An African proverb*

And he said, I have been very jealous for the Lord God of hosts: for the children of Israel have forsaken thy covenant, thrown down thine altars, and slain thy prophets with the sword; and I, even I only, am left; and they seek my life, to take it away. 14 And he said, I have been very jealous for the Lord God of hosts: because the children of Israel have forsaken thy covenant, thrown down thine altars, and slain thy prophets with the sword; and I, even I only, am left; and they seek my life, to take it away. 15 And the Lord said unto him, Go, return on thy way to the wilderness of Damascus: and when thou comest, anoint Hazael to be king over Syria: 16 And Jehu the son of Nimshi shalt thou anoint to be king over Israel: and Elisha the son of Shaphat of Abelmeholah shalt thou anoint to be prophet in thy room. 17 And it shall come to pass, that him that escapeth the sword of Hazael shall Jehu slay: and him that escapeth from the sword of Jehu shall Elisha slay. 18 Yet I have left me seven thousand in Israel, all the knees which have not bowed unto Baal, and every mouth which hath not kissed him. (1 Kings 19:10, 14-18 KJV)

Elijah tells God twice that he has been very jealous for him, and was the only prophet left. He had reached the point of thinking no one else was standing up against the prophets of Baal, and as zealous for God as he was. He had reached a point of deception, and God tells him plainly, "I have left me seven thousand in Israel, all the knees which have not bowed unto Baal."

Please understand that Elijah had just had a great victory, calling down fire from heaven and slaying the prophets of Baal. When we experience great moves of God, we cannot let it go to our heads and deceive us, thinking that we are the only ones experiencing God in such a great way. This is an indication of a lone ranger mentality, and it is a deception every generation must guard against.

Shortly after these comments, God tells Elijah to go and anoint Elisha to stand in his stead. We cannot afford to go alone. A lone ranger mentality will lead us to being replaced. It would have been better if Elijah had had the opportunity to work with 7,000 others. But he did not.

Some in the fathering and mothering generation have a tendency of going alone. They do not allow anyone to come alongside them and they are not mentoring anyone either. This was the case before God instructed Elijah to mentor Elisha.

Samson suffered a similar deception. Though he was the strongest man on earth, he did not learn that he could not make it alone. He was strong, but being a lone ranger got the best of him.

> *...for by strength shall no man prevail. (1 Samuel 2:9b KJV)*

Samson was a great man. The strongest man that ever lived. He could kill a lion with absolutely nothing in his hands. He took the pillars and the gates of an entire city, put them on his shoulders, climbed a hill with them, and threw them off. He was dangerous, but he was a loner.

He walked alone and Delilah, the hired assassin, finished him. It is dangerous to walk alone.

I am extremely concerned and worried about smart people who are alone. When you walk alone, it is not difficult for the enemy to take you out. Samson lacked wisdom and had to learn this lesson the hard way.

The Need for Wisdom

I am worried about this generation. They are smart and intelligent, but not always wise. Knowledge makes you intelligent: It makes you smart. But wisdom makes you wise.

Samson was smart, strong, and skillful, but he was not wise, so he walked alone. He got involved with three women. He married the first woman, and his friend took his wife from him. Then, he went in to see a harlot. Part of his downfall and deception was that he remained anointed, even after he went for a harlot.

The Deception of the Anointed

Don't let the anointing lead you into a "lone ranger" mentality. The issue with the anointing, which this young generation does not understand, is that a person can be anointed and still go around sinning, because the gifts and callings of God are without repentance. God doesn't anoint a person because of their character. The anointing is not given to people based on character; it's given for an assignment. So a person can have bad character and still be anointed. The fact that someone is anointed does not mean God is with, or approves all their behaviors and character. When a person stays with God and lives holy, they carry the presence of God. That is different from the anointing.

If we are like Samson and think we can walk alone because we are anointed, or we think we don't need a father or mother to speak wisdom into our lives, we will be easy prey for the enemy. No matter how anointed we are, we need to be accountable to someone. Samuel needed Eli to train him, even though Eli was getting old, and his eyes were growing dim. The deception of the anointed thinking you do not need a father can cause you to become a spiritual bastard. We must always be able to answer the question, who am I connected to? Who is my father, mother, or mentor? Who am I willing to listen to, be accountable, and submit to?

There's Something Better than the Anointing: It Comes Through Connection

A caution to the anointed is that a person can sin and still be anointed. A person can still be divinely enabled because the gifts and callings of God are without repentance. Another dangerous deception is that, if the focus is only on the applause of men, you can miss something that's more excellent than the anointing, which is the glory of His presence and the wisdom of mentorship.

There is a difference between an anointing, a mantle, and the presence of God. The anointing is a divine enablement of the Spirit to accomplish an assignment or task. A mantle envelopes, clothes, and covers someone to walk in an office or to function in a realm as father, patriarch, or matriarch of a movement. You can have an anointing and not have a mantle and you can have the anointing and lack the presence of God– His abiding presence in, on, and working through your life.

We need to desire the anointing, God's presence, and the mantle. For example, Moses had the anointing, the presence, and the mantle. He also had the presence of his father-in-law giving him wisdom to lead. He could have ignored his father-in-law's counsel because he was a Midianite priest, but he accepted the wisdom of his elder and as a result all of Israel benefitted.

Mantles come through sustained connection with fathers and mothers. If you disconnect from your father or mother, you will likely not receive their mantle. The presence of God comes through sustained connection with the ultimate Father, Yahweh.

When Elijah decide

CHAPTER 7

BRIDGE-BUILDING STRATEGIES AND INSIGHTS

We are at a pivotal moment in history. Across the nations of the world and in various organizations, bridging the gap is the new diversity issue that is causing greater challenges than race or gender diversity. Our major problem is generational diversity. It is not just a church problem. It is a global challenge.

For example, by 2030, young Africans are expected to make up 42% of the world's youth and account for 75% of those under age 35 in Africa. If we don't learn how to bridge the gap, we will have a huge problem on our hands. A large percentage of the world's population would be ill-prepared for the future and Africa would be severely impacted.

The potential for the young generation to impact the world in the coming decade is unprecedented. It is a strategic time for young people to realize and unlock their full potential. They must submit to wisdom and be willing to give what they must to maximize their future. A similar situation ensued in John 6:5-14:

When Jesus looked up and saw a great crowd coming toward him, he said to Philip, "Where shall we buy bread for these people to eat?" 6 He asked this only to test him, for he already had in mind what he was going to do. 7 Philip answered him, "It would take more than half a year's wages[a] to buy enough bread for each one to have a bite!" 8 Another of his disciples, Andrew, Simon Peter's brother, spoke up, 9 "Here is a boy with five small barley loaves and two small fish, but how far will they go among so many?" 10 Jesus said, "Have the people sit down." There was plenty of grass in that place, and they sat down (about five thousand men were there). 11 Jesus then took the loaves, gave thanks, and distributed to those who were seated as much as they wanted. He did the same with the fish. 12 When they had all had enough to eat, he said to his disciples, "Gather the pieces that are left over. Let nothing be wasted." 13 So they gathered them and filled twelve baskets with the pieces of the five barley loaves left over by those who had eaten. 14 After the people saw the sign Jesus performed, they began to say, "Surely this is the Prophet who is to come into the world."

(John 6:5-14 KJV)

The lad was willing to share his fish and bread. He represents a young generation that is willing to share what they have. When he shared the little that he had, it became a blessing to an entire multitude. There are lessons to be learned here. Jesus told them to sit down in groups, there was order and structure. Jesus guided the process. The experience of the older generation is needed to help guide the younger generation and guarantee a sustainable future.

If you are a young man or woman reading this book, you must know that you carry great potential. Do not despise what you have because of how it may look or how you are perceived.

The Bible encourages us not to despise the days of small beginnings, and to not let anyone despise our youth. There were older, middle, and younger-aged generations on that mountain. However, it was the younger generation, the lad, who was willing to give up the five loaves of bread and two fish he had to the disciples and Jesus. As a result, Jesus takes the meal, blesses it, and begins breaking it into pieces. The food kept multiplying until every generation represented in the crowd was full. This means that if the younger generation will not withhold, but release what they have – their talents, abilities, and gifts—God will feed everyone and there will be more than enough. (In the case of the crowd that Jesus fed, there were twelve baskets full of leftovers, for everyone to take home.) The hope of the world is in the next generation, because God has given them something that will change their nations no matter how small it may look. The Israelite babies born during the 40 years of wandering in the desert entered the promised land, and young David who killed Goliath are examples of such hope.

Despite the fact that the next generation have gifts, abilities, and talents, they may not know how to fully develop them. They may not know how to develop their full potential and power. Yet God does and so does the older generation. Working together will result in overflow and the miracle of multiplication.

Each generation brings a different set of expectations and experiences. But we must learn how to work together for the common good to overcome issues such as isolation, demotivation, and low morale that are plaguing the next generation. Saul allowed David to go to battle against Goliath. David was respectful but opted for five smooth stones instead of Saul's armor. The result was an unprecedented victory.

This is why the primary focus of my ministry, for the last few years, has been returning to the schools. This has been a deliberate choice. I have prioritized the emerging generation in our middle and secondary schools, as well as colleges. I could choose to preach on megachurch platforms and on some of the world's biggest stages. But, my priority and passion, now, is the next generation, and honestly that is where I receive the most fulfillment and joy.

Some of Ghana's cutting-edge preachers, like Reverend Eastwood Anaba, Reverend Dr Ampiah Kwofie, Bishop Dag Heward Mills, and Apostle General Sam Korankyi Ankrah and several others, are students who were impacted by my ministry years ago when I visited the high schools. So, we never know who our young generation will become tomorrow. Let us continue investing and we shall see a great harvest.

Each person who reads this book should commit to being a bridge-builder and I want to share some practical insights on how to do so and give strategies for becoming a bridge-builder from the wisdom I have gleaned over the years.

Bridge-builders commit.

First and foremost, if you are of the older generation, commit to giving back by being a mentor. Being a father (or mother) takes commitment. Commit to being a bridge-builder. Like my friend, Bishop T.D. Jakes, has said, it's time for our generation to "leave the stage to become the stage," so we offer opportunities for the emerging generation to discover what is truly in them for the advancement of the kingdom of God.

You must realize that you are not going to lead forever. Someone is coming after you, so why not leave them better off and empower them through your mentorship. You must be intentional and begin by committing time, each week, to pour into others. Make time and take advantage of opportunities. For example, do not eat alone. Invite a mentee to share a meal with you or invite others to join a portion of your workday, so that they can see and participate in your hard work for on-the-job training.

If you have tried to mentor before and felt betrayed by the younger generation, ask the Lord to bring those you are assigned to impact. God spoke to Moses about Joshua. There is someone or some group of people God wants you to mentor. There is a principle in Titus 2:4 that the older women should teach the younger.

2 Timothy 2:2 says, "And the things that thou hast heard of me among many witnesses, the same commit thou to faithful men, who shall be able to teach others also." This is the season for us to become bridge-builders, not those who build walls and tear down bridges, but those who foster unity with a multi-generational mindset.

Bridge-builders overcome fear: do not be afraid to show your scars.

Do not be afraid to show your scars. Fear is the reason why generations don't work together. The older are afraid of the younger generation. That is what happened between Saul and David. The younger generation are also afraid that the older will abuse them or neglect them and take advantage of them.

Throughout the years, I've shared my testimony on campuses and in schools. I have been very transparent. I was a nobody, and my testimony gives the young generation hope. We must not be ashamed to share with the young generation how we started, what we have learned along the way, and what our successes and failures have been. Winston Churchill said, "Success is not final, failure is not fatal. It's the courage to continue that counts."

Despite being ostracized, misrepresented, and rejected, I have continued to share my stories, scars, successes, and lessons learned. When we do this, we keep the younger generation from pitfalls and landmines, and from reinventing the wheel.

> *"From henceforth let no man trouble me: for I bear in my body the marks of the Lord Jesus."*
>
> *Galatians 6 : 17 KJV*

Bridge-builders are kingdom-focused; they reach across lines.

Many of the people I have trained and mentored began in or are still in different denominations. To build bridges, I've been open to working with people from various backgrounds, because God saw something in them that needed to be developed under my leadership. I do not force every person I have mentored to lead in my own denomination. We need to find commonalities. Bridging the gap requires working with people who are not exactly like you and come from different denominations, backgrounds, tribes, ethnicities, and political parties. We must do this without compromising the ancient landmarks and the boundaries of Scripture.

Bridge-builders invest in others.

To bridge the gap, we must invest time in relationship-building, as well as other resources, to develop and mentor others. Sometimes, at great cost I have invested resources in others just to see them become better.

Bridge-builders walk in humility.

We must walk in humility recognizing that we need each other to avoid a curse, which means "programmed to fail." One of the greatest prayers of Jesus is still unanswered for the most part, because we are not willing to make ourselves of no reputation for the greater good of unifying the body of Christ. In John 17: 11, 21...Jesus prayed to the Father to make His disciples one even as He and the Father are one, not just them but all those that will believe on Him through them, that they may be one. Then he said in John 13:35, "By this shall all men know that ye are my disciples, if ye have love one to another." This love causes us to put our differences aside so that what God wants to do on the earth, He can depend on us to get it done together. As you read this, know that you need me, and I need you. God is counting on us to unite! The world must see a triumphant church!

> *"Behold, how good and how pleasant it is For brethren to dwell together in unity! It is like the precious ointment upon the head, that ran down upon the beard, Even Aaron's beard: That went down to the skirts of his garments; As the dew of Hermon, And as the dew that descended upon the mountains of Zion: For there the LORD commanded the blessing, Even life for evermore."*
>
> *Psalm 133 : 1 - 3 KJV*

Building the gap takes time and sacrifice; it doesn't happen overnight.

It takes time, sacrifice, and resources, but it's worth it in the end. Making a decision to bridge the gap will cost us something, but it is worth it. It cost Jesus his life to bridge the gap. Because the price of not sacrificing is an alternative we cannot afford. Bridging the gap is not as easy as it sounds, but we must be intentional to get it done. It will cost us to invest time to mentor those who do not look like us and think like us. We need to make time to answer questions. Like David, we need to make resources available for the younger generation to prepare for the coming move of God. Patience is needed to heal the wounded. Acknowledging our weaknesses, and challenging assumptions and mindsets that don't foster unity is also important.

Bridge-builders are discerning. They don't reject their sons' visions and dreams prematurely.

> *"Jesus saith unto them, did ye never read in the scriptures, The stone which the builders rejected, The same is become the head of the corner: This is the Lord's doing, And it is marvellous in our eyes?"*
>
> *(Matthew 21:42 KJV)*

Fathers must be mindful of how they deal with the dreams of their sons and daughters to make sure that they cover them and support them rather than fight them and reject them. In the days of Jesus, the religious order and the generation that was before Christ, didn't work with Him. Instead, they fought with him and missed out on what he was assigned to do. Without them, He still succeeded, because it was God's blueprint for the salvation of all mankind.

Even today we see how fathers of industry and innovation reject the emerging generations' boldness and eagerness to improve on the works they did. While the National Aeronautics and Space Administration (NASA) partnered, sponsored, mentored, and believed in their astronauts, you would think that some of those same notable astronauts, like Neil Armstrong and Eugene Cernan, would do the same for the next generation. This generation, not unlike them, has a similar audacity, tenacity, and fire to break barriers and chart new territories like they once did in their time. Why not pay it forward to the next generation, mainly because they have inspired the hearts and minds of that young generation, of future astronauts and innovators such as Elon Musk. He is the wealthiest man in the world, who happens to be the owner of Tesla, founder of SpaceEx and new owner of Twitter.

However instead of embracing Elon, who happened to consider them as his heroes and inspiration. they rejected him and forfeited the opportunity to bridge the gap between their generation and his. As a matter of fact, they predicted his downfall, and declared that he would become a burden to the American taxpayer. They took their issue to NASA and to the United States Congress, where they accused him and berated him. However, after many unnecessary struggles, failures, and setbacks, Elon continued forward and eventually prevailed. His company has built an entirely new industry that has unlimited potential for jobs, national wealth, and the advancement of mankind. What they rejected out of hubris, pride, and insecurity, has now become a force to be reckoned with. They missed the opportunity to be celebrated around the world, while enjoying the success from collaboration and mentorship. Instead of being celebrated as fathers who passed on the baton of innovation and ingenuity and shared knowledge, they chose to reject him and forever be seen as relics of the past. They have, unfortunately, missed it.

This is why fathers must be discerning like Jacob. When Joseph shared a complex dream that shifted the order of things, Jacob did not understand, but he listened and partnered with Joseph standing steadfast for the manifestation of his dream. This was markedly different from the approach his brothers took, which was instead, to design a nefarious plot to kill him for his dream. The irony of it all, is that the dream happened as he had seen it. However, their lives depended on it happening exactly the way Joseph dreamt it. Therefore, fathers must always be discerning, working with the younger generations and not brushing them aside as lightweights or insignificant.

Every generation must be bridge-builders. It works both ways.

The younger generation that respects and chooses to walk on the bridge the elders built, must harness themselves to the path by committing to focus. Just as Elijah said to Elisha, "if you see me go, then you will receive a double portion of my spirit.". So, no matter what kind of turbulent winds, tornados, or hurricanes Elijah's ascension caused on the earth, Elisha kept his eyes focused on him. This is the condition the fulfillment of his request was built on. He had to keep his eyes open to see his father being taken up. Then and only then, would he receive the blessing of the ancient landmark. By God's grace, Elisha succeeded, and the mantle became his.

Many generations later, Peter had a similar opportunity. He saw Jesus, walking on the water.

> *"And Peter answered him and said, Lord, if it be thou, bid me come unto thee on the water. And he said, Come. And when Peter was come down out of the ship, he walked on the water, to go to Jesus. But when he saw the wind boisterous, he was afraid; and beginning to sink, he cried, saying, Lord, save me."*
>
> *(Matthew 14 :28 -30 KJV)*

The word "Come" was the infrastructure that bridged the gap. Before he said "Come" there was no bridge. Peter, who is the younger generation, needed a bridge to get to Jesus, so when he was permitted, he quickly obliged and began to do something no other man beside Jesus had done before...walk on water! He was not able to do it by His own strength, wisdom, or might. It was by his focus. Focus is the thrust and energy that keeps you moving forward on the bridge.

However, Peter began to do what many of the younger generation do, he began to focus on the gap, instead of the bridge. The gap represents the circumstances, fears, threats, struggles, offenses, difficulties, or in other words, simply put, distractions.

Distraction is the archenemy of the one who walks on the bridge. Distraction will lead you into deep violent waters of regret and major setback. By the grace of God, some recover, but many unfortunately never do.

I celebrate Peter because he had the wherewithal to cry out, "LORD save me!". Some children will never cry out, because of guilt or shame. Look at Adam and Eve in the garden. After they ate the forbidden fruit, the Bible tells us that they hid.

> *"And they heard the voice of the LORD God walking in the garden in the cool of the day:*

> *and Adam and his wife hid themselves from the presence of the LORD God amongst the trees of the garden."*
>
> *Genesis 3 :8 KJV*

Now fathers, congratulations for building the bridge and congratulations for having a son or a daughter willing to walk on that bridge. Never be in a rush to condemn, but always be in a rush to save and protect.

> *"But when he saw the wind boisterous, he was afraid; and beginning to sink, he cried, saying, Lord, save me. And immediately Jesus stretched forth his hand, and caught him, and said unto him, O thou of little faith, wherefore didst thou doubt?"*
>
> *Matthew 14 :30 -31 KJV*

A good father will always rush to the cry of their child.

For instance, even though Abraham mentored Lot for many years and helped develop him to the point where he flourished economically, Lot still made countless mistakes. He chose the best land and left the less fertile land to his uncle. He failed to show appreciation for all of Abraham's sacrifices for him, and eventually chose to live separate from him, after he had lost everything.

In the battle of the Kings, Abraham rescued Lot and all his possessions.

> *"And he brought back all the goods, and also brought again his brother Lot, and his goods, and the women also, and the people."*
>
> *Genesis 14 :16 KJV*

When Sodom was about to be destroyed, Abraham negotiated Lot's safe passage and deliverance. This is a mentor's heart. This is the heart of a father, a mother, and mentor, interceding and negotiating with God for the release, redemption, and total freedom of the children under their care. Even though Abraham did everything to save and protect Lot, a father cannot force a child back onto the bridge. If he or she returns to the bridge, only their focus can keep them there.

At times, the younger generation can be too quick to want to see sudden or immediate change or activity, not realizing that all things are done in Gods' timing. Sometimes their covering might follow a blueprint and particular pattern that they cannot see or understand.

For instance, on the Mount of transfiguration, Peter tries to bridge the gap that is not his to bridge.

"And after six days Jesus taketh with him Peter, and James, and John, and leadeth them up into an high mountain apart by themselves: and he was transfigured before them. And his raiment became shining, exceeding white as snow; so as no fuller on earth can white them. And there appeared unto them Elias with Moses: and they were talking with Jesus. And Peter answered and said to Jesus, Master, it is good for us to be here: and let us make three tabernacles; one for thee, and one for Moses, and one for Elias. For he wist not what to say; for they were sore afraid." Genesis 14:2-6

Sometimes being silent and waiting on the father, mother or mentor is the wisest position a child could ever take. Peter was trying to bridge the gap between Jesus, Moses and Elijah. However, God the Father quickly puts him in his place.

Genesis 14:7

"And there was a cloud that overshadowed them: and a voice came out of the cloud, saying, This is my beloved Son: hear him."

In other words, Peter you may know that Moses represents the Law and Elijah the prophets, but Jesus My Son has fulfilled them both. His covenant is greater than theirs and he is, not only the bridge for Peter, James and John's, also a bridge for Moses' and Elijah. No matter what you see My Son go through, do not try to create or do anything yourself. He is the Way, the Truth and the Life. In other words, shut up and listen to Him!

Bridge-builders, both young and old, understand that God wants to use the young generation.

The older generation needs to believe that God wants to and can use young people. At the same time, the young generation needs to believe in themselves. There are so many examples of God using young people to achieve great things.

The boy Samuel ministered before the Lord. 1 Samuel 2:18

- Wolfgang Amadeus Mozart created his first musical composition at five years of age. (www.britannica.com/biography/Wolfgang-Amadeus-Mozart)

- Zuriel Oduwole became the youngest person in the world, at 10, to be featured for her advocacy work in Forbes magazine. As a filmmaker and girls education advocate, she made her first documentary about the Ghana Revolution at age nine.(zurieloduwole.com)

- Pablo Picasso painted his first work of art by nine years. (www.co.hunterdon.nj.us)

- Stevie Wonder, who has been blind since childhood, learned how to play the keyboard, the harmonica, and the drums, and recorded his first album at twelve years old. (www.biography.

com/muscian/stevie-wonder)

- Human rights advocate and humanitarian Eddie Ndopu will be the first person with a disability to travel to space, making history, as the youngest United Nations Sustainable Development Goal Advocate(SDG) and the first African with a disability to have graduated from Oxford University before 30.(unsdgadvocates.org/edward-ndopu)

- It is believed that David was twelve years old when he was first anointed to be King. And he was a youth when he volunteered to fight Goliath

- The prophet Jeremiah was ordained from his mother's womb. Jeremiah 1:5

- It is commonly believed that Mary, the mother of Jesus, was in her teens when she carried the son of God.

- Patricia Mawuli became Ghana's first female civilian pilot and the first West African to build and maintain Rotax engines. (www.flourishafrica.com)

- When Ishmael was dying with his mother in the wilderness, God made provision for them when he heard the cry of the child. Genesis 21:17

- In 1963, African American children participated

in the Birmingham Children's Crusade, a school walk out to march in protest for Civil Rights. (www.zinnedproject.org)

- Paul told Timothy let no man despise your youth. 1 Timothy 4:12

- God said, in the last days, he would pour out his spirit upon all flesh. Joel 2:28

- Without a doubt, God wants to use the young and emerging generation. Let us resolve to be bridge-builders, to bridge the gap, so the next generation can fulfill their potential.

> *"Out of the mouth of babes and sucklings hast thou ordained strength because of thine enemies, That thou mightest still the enemy and the avenger."*
>
> *Psalm 8 : 2 KJV*

The strategic bridge of transgenerational prayers

The mystery and power of prayer is that the lips that prayed may be sealed and no longer alive, however, the prayers live on and may be working so potently and powerfully, regardless of space and time. One powerful example of this today is the prayers of Solomon. People still go to Jerusalem to pray.

The prayers of Jesus after over two thousand years

are still very effective even today. Long after David was dead, the Queen of Sheba arose in response to the prayers of a dead father and traveled 1,500 miles on camels to bring gold and incense with spices from Ethiopia to Jerusalem to bless Solomon.

Let us deploy this time-tested strategy as a bridge to cover many generations and to bless our nations, ministries, churches, businesses, to engage and covenant with the God of many generations to bring it to pass. May the Lord richly bless you and continue to use you mightily as His battle axe and weapons of war to establish his kingdom and will in the earth for generations in Jesus mighty name.

May the prayers of the lips that are sealed and lying silent in eternity live on, working as an unstoppable force and power in time, bringing to pass what was prayed and echoed before the throne of grace.

DAVID'S PRAYER

Psalm 72

King James Version

> 1 *Give the king thy judgments, O God, and thy righteousness unto the king's son.*
>
> 2 *He shall judge thy people with righteousness,*

and thy poor with judgment.

3 The mountains shall bring peace to the people, and the little hills, by righteousness.

4 He shall judge the poor of the people, he shall save the children of the needy, and shall break in pieces the oppressor.

5 They shall fear thee as long as the sun and moon endure, throughout all generations.

6 He shall come down like rain upon the mown grass: as showers that water the earth.

7 In his days shall the righteous flourish; and abundance of peace so long as the moon endureth.

8 He shall have dominion also from sea to sea, and from the river unto the ends of the earth.

9 They that dwell in the wilderness shall bow before him; and his enemies shall lick the dust.

10 The kings of Tarshish and of the isles shall bring presents: the kings of Sheba and Seba shall offer gifts.

11 Yea, all kings shall fall down before him: all nations shall serve him.

12 For he shall deliver the needy when he crieth; the poor also, and him that hath no helper.

13 He shall spare the poor and needy, and shall save the souls of the needy.

14 He shall redeem their soul from deceit and violence: and precious shall their blood be in his sight.

15 And he shall live, and to him shall be given of the gold of Sheba: prayer also shall be made for him continually; and daily shall he be praised.

16 There shall be an handful of corn in the earth upon the top of the mountains; the fruit thereof shall shake like Lebanon: and they of the city shall flourish like grass of the earth.

17 His name shall endure for ever: his name shall be continued as long as the sun: and men shall be blessed in him: all nations shall call him blessed.

18 Blessed be the Lord God, the God of Israel, who only doeth wondrous things.

19 And blessed be his glorious name for ever: and let the whole earth be filled with his glory; Amen, and Amen.

20 The prayers of David the son of Jesse are ended.

PRAYER FOR SARAH

GENESIS 17:15

15 And God said unto Abraham, As for Sarai thy wife, thou shalt not call her name Sarai, but Sarah shall her name be.

16 And I will bless her, and give thee a son also of her: yea, I will bless her, and she shall be a mother of nations; kings of people shall be of her.

17 Then Abraham fell upon his face, and laughed, and said in his heart, Shall a child be born unto him that is an hundred years old? and shall Sarah, that is ninety years old, bear?

18 And Abraham said unto God, O that Ishmael might live before thee!

19 And God said, Sarah thy wife shall bear thee a son indeed; and thou shalt call his name Isaac: and I will establish my covenant with him for an everlasting covenant, and with his seed after him.

20 And as for Ishmael, I have heard thee: Behold, I have blessed him, and will make him fruitful, and will multiply him exceedingly; twelve princes shall he beget, and I will make him a great nation.

[21] But my covenant will I establish with Isaac, which Sarah shall bear unto thee at this set time in the next year.

JESUS PRAYS FOR HIS DISCIPLES

JOHN 17: 6-19

*[6] "I have revealed you[a] to those whom you gave
me out of the world. They were yours; you gave
them to me and they have obeyed your word. [7]
Now they know that everything you have given
me comes from you. [8] For I gave them the words
you gave me and they accepted them. They knew
with certainty that I came from you, and they
believed that you sent me. [9] I pray for them. I am
not praying for the world, but for those you have
given me, for they are yours. [10] All I have is yours,
and all you have is mine. And glory has come to
me through them. [11] I will remain in the world no
longer, but they are still in the world, and I am
coming to you. Holy Father, protect them by the
power of[b] your name, the name you gave me,
so that they may be one as we are one. [12] While I
was with them, I protected them and kept them
safe by[c] that name you gave me. None has
been lost except the one doomed to destruction
so that Scripture would be fulfilled.*

[13] "I am coming to you now, but I say these things
while I am still in the world, so that they may
have the full measure of my joy within them. 14
I have given them your word and the world has
hated them, for they are not of the world any
more than I am of the world. [15] My prayer is not
that you take them out of the world but that you
protect them from the evil one. [16] They are not
of the world, even as I am not of it. [17] Sanctify
them by[d] the truth; your word is truth. [18] As you
sent me into the world, I have sent them into the
world. [19] For them I sanctify myself, that they too
may be truly sanctified.

JESUS PRAYS FOR HIS BELIEVERS

JOHN 17:20-26

[20] "My prayer is not for them alone. I pray also
for those who will believe in me through their
message, [21] that all of them may be one, Father,
just as you are in me and I am in you. May they
also be in us so that the world may believe that
you have sent me. [22] I have given them the glory
that you gave me, that they may be one as we
are one— [23] I in them and you in me—so that
they may be brought to complete unity. Then
the world will know that you sent me and have
loved them even as you have loved me.

[24] "Father, I want those you have given me to be with me where I am, and to see my glory, the glory you have given me because you loved me before the creation of the world.

[25] "Righteous Father, though the world does not know you, I know you, and they know that you have sent me. [26] I have made you[e] known to them, and will continue to make you known in order that the love you have for me may be in them and that I myself may be in them."

Solomon Prays at the Temple

(1 Kings 8.22-53)

12-13 Earlier, Solomon had a bronze platform made that was about two meters square and over a meter high, and he put it in the center of the outer courtyard near the altar. Solomon stood on the platform facing the altar with everyone standing behind him. Then he lifted his arms toward heaven; he knelt down 14 and prayed:

Lord God of Israel, no other god in heaven or on earth is like you!

You never forget the agreement you made with your people, and you are loyal to anyone who faithfully obeys your teachings. 15 My father David was your servant, and today you have kept every promise you made to him.

16 (B) You promised that someone from his family would always be king of Israel, if they do their best to obey you, just as he did. 17 Please keep this promise you made to your servant David. 18 (C) There's not enough room in all of heaven for you, Lord God. How could you possibly live on earth in this temple I have built? 19 But I ask you to answer my prayer. 20 (D) This is the temple where you have chosen to be worshiped. Please watch over it day and night and listen when I turn toward it and pray. 21 I am your servant, and the people of Israel belong to you, and so whenever any of us look toward this temple and pray, answer from your home in heaven and forgive our sins.

22 Suppose someone accuses a person of a crime, and the accused has to stand in front of the altar in your temple and say, "I swear I am innocent!" 23 Listen from heaven and decide who is right. Then punish the guilty person and let the innocent one go free.

24 Suppose your people Israel sin against you, and then an enemy defeats them. If they come to this temple and beg for forgiveness, 25 listen from your home in heaven. Forgive them and bring them back to the land you gave their ancestors.

26 Suppose your people sin against you, and

you punish them by holding back the rain. If they stop sinning and turn toward this temple to pray in your name, 27 listen from your home in heaven and forgive them. The people of Israel are your servants, so teach them to live right. And send rain on the land you promised them forever.

28 Sometimes the crops may dry up or rot or be eaten by locusts[a] or grasshoppers, and your people will be starving. Sometimes enemies may surround their towns, or your people will become sick with deadly diseases. 29 Please listen when anyone in Israel truly feels sorry and sincerely prays with arms lifted toward your temple. 30 You know what is in everyone's heart. So from your home in heaven answer their prayers, according to what they do and what is in their hearts. 31 Then your people will worship you and obey you for as long as they live in the land you gave their ancestors.

32 Foreigners will hear about you and your mighty power, and some of them will come to live among your people Israel. If any of them pray toward this temple, 33 listen from your home in heaven and answer their prayers. Then everyone on earth will worship you, just as your own people Israel do, and they will know that I have built this temple in your honor.

34 Sometimes you will order your people to attack their enemies. Then your people will turn toward this temple I have built for you in your chosen city, and they will pray to you. 35 Answer their prayers from heaven and give them victory.

36 Everyone sins. But when your people sin against you, suppose you get angry enough to let their enemies drag them away to foreign countries. 37-39 Later, they may feel sorry for what they did and ask your forgiveness. Answer them when they pray toward this temple I have built for you in your chosen city, here in this land you gave their ancestors. From your home in heaven, listen to their sincere prayers and forgive your people who have sinned against you.

40 Lord God, hear us when we pray in this temple. 41 (E) Come to your new home, where we have already placed the sacred chest, which is the symbol of your strength. I pray that when the priests announce your power to save people, those who are faithful to you will celebrate what you've done for them. 42 Always remember the love you had for your servant David,[b] so that you will not reject your chosen kings

Remember:

- Bridge-builders provide easy passage for the next generation.

- Bridge-builders become icons. The next generation reveres and celebrates them, even if the people of their day do not understand them and they are misrepresented.

- Bridge-builders become a necessity in challenging and difficult times when a special kind of leadership is required.

- Bridge-builders intercede, pray and make declarations to preserve the posterity of the emerging generation

With over four decades of Ministry behind him, Archbishop Nicholas Duncan- Williams is the Presiding Archbishop and General Overseer of Christian Action Faith Ministries (CAFM). CAFM has over 150 affiliate and branch churches located in North America, Europe, Asia and Africa. Archbishop Duncan-Williams is also the Founder and President of Prayer Summit International and Global Prayer Invasion, which bring the message and the Power of Prayer to many around the world.

With a unique anointing in the area of prayer and intercession, Archbishop has been recognized by many leaders in the body of Christ as the "Apostle of Strategic Prayer"

Having gained accreditation and respect by various church leaders, God has used him to counsel and speak into the lives of world leaders, while still maintaining his touch with the common man. He is affectionately called "Papa" by many.